Financially Lit

Upcoming release by Dale H. Ferdinand

The Science Of Closing A Deal

The Ferocious Salesman

Taking Massive Action

Level Up

Be Extraordinary and Stay Relentless

Chronicles Of A Closer

Financially Lit

How to supersize your income

Written by

Dale H. Ferdinand

Contents

Introduction 1
Chapter 1: Stop dreaming and get to it 4
Chapter 2: Be careful where you get your advice 9
Chapter 3: Get your mind right 13
Chapter 4: Do the math, to get the cash 18
Chapter 5: Increase your cash flow 22
Chapter 6: The money is already printed, you just have to go and get it 30
Chapter 7: Don't let your money just sit around 39
Chapter 8: Just saving money is a losing strategy 47
Chapter 9: More streams equals more success 54
Chapter 10: Repetition is the mission 60
About the author 69

Introduction

This is Financially lit: How to supersize your income and I am the author Dale H. Ferdinand. I did not write this book to be one of the best-written books of all time. Or to use a bunch of saying that leave you scratching your head and wondering what I mean and clueless on how to apply these lessons into your life right away. I wrote this book in a simple and easy to read way, that will give you a clear and easy path to take action right away and supersize your income. This book will serve as your step by step platform to become financially lit and gain massive wealth. Financially lit is the term that was made famous by Jay Morrison. However, lit comes from the Latin word ignite, which means to obtain an extraordinary level of financial freedom and to ignite your economic fire within you to succeed continuously. My sole purpose in this life is to motivate and inspire mass amounts of people, who then follow my lead and gain wealth and truly change the quality of life and mentality of the people around them.

I was inspired to write this book after having a conversation with my 8-year-old daughter about her goals and how she can achieve them. My daughter replied two things to me. Number one that she wanted to be rich and number two that she wanted to be famous for being rich. I then said to her, those sound like two magnificent goals baby. Have you told anyone else about these goals? She said yes, she told her teacher and her entire class, then one of her classmates told her that his parents told him that being rich and famous isn't important in life.

Instead, that they should just work hard in school, get a good job and just be happy with what she has. I replied to my daughter that you couldn't expect a rabbit to understand how an eagle thinks.

Now, I know what you are thinking, what do I mean by that. The rabbit and the eagle have two completely different missions and views on life. The rabbit can only see but so far ahead of him and behind him, while the eagle can see miles ahead of him at a time. The reason the Eagles see a better view is because the eagle flies high. Here it is at the tender age of 8, my daughter's classmate has already been sold on not maximizing his efforts to achieve his highest potential in life. He has already been sold on not trying to set a new standard for himself and potentially his future family. This was a prime example of being broke mentally; This is the poison that is pushed onto our children and to even some adults, which trains them to have a can't do mentality. Which I'm more than willing to say was pushed on me as well during my life.

Not only did I tell my daughter that her goals were amazing, I told her why would you stop there? The look of excitement that was on my daughter's face as her eyes widen was priceless. I then ask her okay, now what's your game plan to get there? I then said that you must first have a product to sell and a story to tell. In one breath, she replied, well in school we read books every day so she could write a book and get rich as she sat laughing and rubbing her hands together. I said okay tremendous but just because you write a book doesn't mean you're going to get rich, you still have to go out there and sell your book. Now how will you sell your book? If you want to make millions of dollars, you need to solve the problems of millions of people. She 'sat there tapping her finger on her chin for about 10 seconds and then she opened up her mouth and said well if I write a book on "how to stop bullying" I can sale that to every school in the world because every school has bullies or someone who has been bullied before. Not only did my daughter come up with a goal, but she also came up with a plan to take action and achieve that goal.

She came up with a strategy that showed the features, advantages and the benefits of her product to her target consumer. My daughter is now in the publishing stage of her first book and will be a published author before her 9th birthday. Whether you are eight years old or 80 years old it all comes down to your ability to visualize and commit to your success.

Chapter 1: Stop dreaming and get to it

Getting rich or even super-sizing your income isn't impossible it is an actual reality. Most importantly no formal education in school or college will teach you how to become a millionaire or show you how to become rich. It is funny how I spent a bunch of time in school and not once learn anything about how money works or how to supersize my income. Instead, I was taught the proper way to read and write. History, science, math and how to dissect a frog. Seriously, how to cut open a frog. Society trains the mass population to make finances or money something that is considered taboo something that is not discussed publicly. In fact, just having ambition and having the drive and wanting to succeed and achieve more in life is frowned on.

I remember watching the Occupy Wall Street movement. Now people are entitled to feel how they want and to have their opinion or whatever they want. As for me, I couldn't quite understand what the protest was about or their message, however, it did shed some light on how society and massive amounts of people were demonizing and frowning upon successful people for being successful. Rather than criticize some of the most successful people on this planet I decided to study them. I began searching to find out what was vital to their success and then copy what worked for them and implement that into my life immediately.

I grew up in a neighborhood of Brooklyn, and the lessons I learned in school did not prepare me for the financial world. I went to college expecting to find out how the world of business, finance worked and the importance of money. How to generate my own income and be financially free. I was consistently pitched by my peers, my teachers, professors, friends, classmates, parents, cousins, aunts and uncles a middle-class non-workable outdated fantasy that the sooner I give up on myself and stop trying to reach my maximum potential and accept being average the better off that I would be. I have traveled from many different places in my life from being at rock bottom to attending American Military University with a major in Entrepreneurship. I have also held various positions in my career from working as a team leader, senior account manager, chief revenue officer, co-founder, chief executive officer, sales trainer and securities trader at many financial services companies and start-ups. As of today, I run two successful companies. Those businesses being DHF Capital Securities, which is an investment management, and proprietary trading company. Also, Ferdinand Training Advisors a virtual sales education, training and consulting company.

When I was writing this book, it wasn't with the intent to brag about my achievements but to reach out to people who believe that they deserve to be financially successful but think that getting rich and super-sizing your income is limited to celebrities, athletes, entertainers, actors, and rappers. I'm here to tell you that it's not. The first thing that you must do is to make a conscious decision to supersize your income. I spend several years in my life just living from week to week and check-to-check until I made a conscious decision to gain financial success for my family and me.

There are many different myths about super-rich people and millionaires. Millionaires come from all different walks of life. They come in all different shapes, sizes, background, and professions. In fact, 80% of millionaires today generate their income from working for someone else. The number one reason people never supersize their pay is that they don't have the vision to know that it is actually possible for them to do so. There are convinced by the people around them just too accept their current financial situation and believe that everything will just be okay. The second reason people don't supersize their income is that they just don't understand money. They don't know how money works. They don't understand that even if you lack having money you can use things such as your credit as leverage to make money and or supersize your income. Right here in America which is one of the wealthiest countries in the world and a superpower, the majority of the citizens in the US are living paycheck to paycheck, are in debt, can't save any money, let alone, know how to multiply the money that they already have.

One of the best pieces of knowledge I acquired while working on Wall Street is that you will never, I repeat, you will never get wealthy or supersize your income by saving money. Here in the US people pride themselves on taking lousy advice when it comes to money. Just look at the financial news media, you got analyst, hedge fund managers, news anchors, pedaling wrong financial information and advice to the masses, and the crazy thing is, that people actually buy into it. For example, If you cook at home rather than eat out, you'll save enough money to do what you want in life. Hey, little Jorge, put your money in the CD account, and if the bank gives you .0001% in 50 years or 60 years, you'll generate enough interest to supersize your income. I'm here to tell you that that is complete bullshit.

The only thing that will happen if you put your money in the CD account for 50 or 60 years at .0001% is that you're going to be 50 years older and still broke. Other people say hey if you just live debt free and live within your means, then you'll be just fine. Or another one is this never borrows money, never use a credit card because these things add up to bad debt. Again I am here to tell you that this is complete bull shit. These financial advisers hop on TV, news media, press, social media the internet and push this wrong information to the masses. They Overlook the fact that all of the super wealthy and individuals who supersize their income do this by using other people's money also known as credit or borrow money and then generate returns on that capital which is known as leverage, more than whatever the interest is on that money that they borrow. If you ask the person nearest to you more than likely, they'll feed you the same advice that they received, go to school, get a good job, buy a house and you should be okay. Anything other than that pray to God and leave it in the Lord's hand. Let me debunk this for you, buying a single family house is a lousy investment. I repeat, buying a home to live in is a bad investment. Now if you buy a multifamily property that has excellent cash-flow that's something entirely different, and I'll save that for another book and go into more details.

When I was growing up, I was broke. In fact, my family was so broke that we had to save up to reach being poor. Growing up under these type of circumstances I wanted nothing more in life than to be rich and have financial freedom. I didn't want just to be okay, I didn't want just to get by, I didn't want to just live from check to check. I realize that the people with the most money were the people who actually decided to go out there and get it. I wanted to supersize my income to the point where no single action could ever make me without money again. So that's what I did.

Chapter 2: Be careful where you get your advice

In life, you must be cautious where you get your advice. This is what I want you to do; I want you to go to your friends and your family and say I'm going to supersize my income to the point that being broke and not having money will be nothing more than a distant memory. If your friends are family are anything like my friends and family was when I first got started on my quest to super-sizing my income I'm pretty sure at least one of them I tell you, yeah right. Expanding on that, I remember when I first made the decision to supersize my income, and I told my father that I was going to start my own business which at the time was an ATM machine and ATM consulting company. His reply was, sure, I'm going to make some space in the basement for your ATMs once that doesn't work out for you. He later then told me why even waste my time trying to become an entrepreneur. Your best option is just to work a job save up some money and stay away from anything risky. Why don't I just follow his footsteps? That I shouldn't waste my time and my money trying to buy dangerous things like properties or invest in the stock market.

He then said that he would rather save his money and keep it in his bank account where he knows his money is safe. Look the worst thing that you can do is save money just for the hack of saving it. The only reason that you should safe money is, so you can then later invest that money and multiply it. So without following my father's instructions, I was able to start up an ATM placement company. I would go out go business-to-business, door to door of business owners with a copy of one of my brochures in my hand and pitch the business owner on how it would benefit their business by having one of my ATM's in their store. I later was able to negotiate with my distributor away that I get the ATM machines up front, without using any money out of my pocket, along with getting a money supply service to replenish my ATM machines for me. All without using any of my money. I went from having two ATM machines in Brooklyn to having hundreds of ATM machines throughout the Tri-State area. That's New York, New Jersey, and Connecticut.

    See if I listen to my dad and other naysayers at the time I would have never been able to complete this task of starting my own business. That's why you must be very selected where you take your advice. Now, was my dad wrong absolutely not, he was just going by what he learned coming up from his personal experiences and with his middle-class mentality. See my dad was originally born in Haiti and came over to the United States as a young child. My grandfather even though he was a successful businessman in Haiti, and ran a very lucrative rice business when he came over to the US he didn't share that information with my dad on entrepreneurship, his only advice for my dad was for him to go to school and get a job.

    My dad worked hard his whole life to take care of my mom, my sister and I. My dad worked two jobs for 30 years and often at times we still found ourselves worrying about money. Growing up under these devastating circumstances, I wanted nothing more than to be able to provide for my family. I hated worrying about money; I hated not having the options to do as we felt whenever we felt like doing something. I remember speaking to my grandfather, and I said, hey grandpa, You know one day your grandson it's going to be extremely rich, and I'm going to help a lot of people. My grandfather said to me, well you know your father used to say the same thing and brushed me off.

After having this conversation with my grandfather, something about his reaction stuck out to me. Something happened in my Dad's life that made him give up on money, and I vowed to myself that I wouldn't let the same thing happen to me. Since then, I consume every type of information regarding wealth, finance, business development, sales, building credit, real estate, mergers and acquisitions and most of all leveraged buyouts. Super-sizing your income is one of the most vital things to your survival on this planet.

Every day you are faced with financial transactions or financial obligations that you must maintain to survive anyone who tells you anything different is a liar. From things like going to the grocery store, or feeding yourself, or going to the laundromat, or taking care of your family or even planning a vacation for your loved ones. These are all financial transactions that take place on the day to the day, in life and sometimes dealing with money limitations or setbacks. See when you're brought up in the middle-class overtime you developed this middle-class mentality, these middle-class ideas, this middle-class decision-making process. I'm here to tell you that the number-one difference between being middle-class and being poor is, absolutely nothing. In fact being middle-class is the new version of being poor.

When it comes to money, economics, and financial freedom it's a lot simpler than a lot of these schools, financial gurus and TV analyst make it out to be. For example, has anyone ever said to you well you can't miss something that you never had (In reference to money)? Nine times out of 10, the person who says statements like this never had enough money to know if it would or if it wouldn't anyway. People use comments like this to justify their current living conditions instead of using this as fuel to feed the fire that's burning inside of them to go out and achieve financial freedom.

This is a prime example of what people do that get stuck so much on the day-to-day, week-to-week of what they're doing just to survive, that they subconsciously put their beliefs, thoughts, and mentality on to you. Now back to that statement that you can't miss anything that you never had. Now I know for some people this may be true, But I would much rather make enough money to find out if it's true or not for myself. One additional note on this. Super-sizing your income is 70% mental preparation and 30% execution.

Chapter 3: Get your mind right

As I said, earlier the biggest mistake that people make when choosing to supersize their income is that they never get their mind right. They never get their mind right and make a conscious decision to supersize their income. In fact, they don't even think it's possible. The idea that you 'just need enough' money to live off is ridiculous. The very first thing you must unquestionably do is get your mind right and make the decision to supersize your income. Once you have decided to supersize your income, you have to set a target for yourself whether it's to become a millionaire, a multimillionaire or even a billionaire it all starts with you getting your mind right and making a decision to get to it.

Once you make that decision, you must reinforce it day in and day out. You have to make a claim in the game. If you say today that I'm going to supersize my income, I promise I will not judge you. In truth, I'll congratulate you on taking the first step in super-sizing your income. If you tell any person who is successful who have supersized their income that you're looking to do the same they would most likely say, excellent, you deserve it; you can do. People who have created wealth and super-sized their income fully understand that it is genuinely a great journey that anyone can do. Keep in mind that 4 out of 5 millionaires are first generation millionaires. Meaning that they have created their incomes by their self.

Meaning that they didn't inherit or acquire their money

from mommy and daddy. I'm not talking about trust fund babies or people who hit the DNA lottery. Now, lets hold on for one second, before you start to say, well Dale I don't want to be rich or supersize my income I just want to be happy. You have to understand two things. Point number one, super-sizing your income isn't only about you. Point number two is that limiting yourself in any aspect of your life undermines your real potential and abilities. Look most of us grew up and was thought to be happy with the bare minimum. Don't want too much in life. That all we need to survive is a house, a car, clothes, food, a decent job, maybe middle to upper management, a few dollars in the bank and go on a vacation once or twice a year. This is what is known as the middle-class. The middle class is for people who decided to settle with just enough to get by rather than make every effort to get wealthy. Settling for the middle class is the most selfish compromises that you could make. When you compromise your finances and income, you then commit yourself to a lifetime of the struggles of the selfish. You suddenly become incapable of helping those around you because you're struggling to take care of yourself. This adds to the constant undermining of who you are.

    You are 100% capable of more than you know. So why would you ever limit yourself to such subpar financial goals for yourself and your family? For my entire life, I have always had this logical thought in the back of my mind, and this feeling in the pit of my stomach, which was knowing that I could do more. Achieve more, give more, help more, work harder, be a better leader, be a father, be a friend and be a better provider. Over time I realize that I'm the most content, overjoyed and upbeat when am maximizing my efforts in pursuit of my goals. I'm also aware that I'm the most unhappy when I not actively and aggressively pursuing my goals. You could make 60k a year or 600k a year and still struggle that all depends on the where you live, your cost of living and the level of responsibility that you have. Also, another thing that you must keep in mind, is that just because someone is doing better than you, doesn't mean that they are better than you.

People always say well at least you didn't grow up in a 3rd world country, that I should be grateful that I have a cell phone, internet, running water and a flush toilet just be happy with that. This is an argument that people make. The truth is, this is just another way for people to tell you to be comfortable with your position in life. See I can't just be comfortable if I am not thriving and perform at my highest levels in all aspects of my life. See I grew up as a firm believer in common sense and in this day and age common sense isn't too common. Trying to make sense out of limiting yourself financially and not having enough money is the absolute most senseless thing you could do. Just even considering not having enough money is insane. Or just thinking that having just enough to be comfortable is ridiculous.

See society trick people into believing into joining the middle class as if it's something that is very prominent honorable and a great life decision and in all actuality, it isn't. You have to ignore all of the naysayers, all of the disbelievers, and all of the people around you who are sold on this middle-class mentality and make a decision to supersize your income. See because you got two choices in life. You can be a thermometer, or you could be a thermostat. A thermometer just reflects the temperature of the environment around it. Well the thermostat sets the temperature and creates the environment. If you were looking to find the treasure, you're going to need a treasure map. If you have a destination that you're trying to reach, you have to use your GPS, and your internal GPS that you have, is your mind, and you have to get your mind right. People get comfortable with temporary things. Some people get comfortable with a decent house, a couple of cars, IRA or even a 401k but spend their life stressed and worried about money. The first step you must take to supersize your income you have to get your mind right. You have to decide to ignore the bad and outdated middle-class mentality. After you do so and you get rid of your middle-class attitude, you have to reorganize your way of thinking.

You have to set larger targets for yourself and think like a millionaire, shit well hell, you need to think like a billionaire. We have to get rid of the small-minded defensive, take no risk mindset. In business, I learned the safest thing to do is to take risks. Entrepreneurs, record breakers, and world shakers don't find success, sitting back being careful and comfortable. They acquire success when their feet are right up at the edge with their toes dangling.

In today's world of technology, smartphones, and the internet it has never been easier for people to supersize their income than it is right now. There are over 75 trillion dollars that's in circulation around this planet each day. However, you wouldn't be able to make your first thousand, hundred thousand or even your first million if you don't break away from your middle-class mind. You have to start the process of building your millionaire mentality. Yeah, and of course I know that plenty of people will disagree with me. Check this out, the people who are not making enough money simply just make sense of why they are not making enough money. In all actuality, being a millionaire today is the new middle-class.

Quite frankly, I know some millionaires that are still struggling. Start using the power of your mind to confirm your ability to supersize your income. However, make the decision right now to do so and when you do so, remember to help the people around you. If you ever start to get low or morale or to start doubting that you can supersize your income, I want you to take out this book and reread it. The only thing you have to do is trust me and believe me; I want you to get there. Sometimes you may not have the confidence in yourself to get to that next level. I know that I didn't, so I put my faith, trust, and belief in the process and applied massive pressure and ferocious levels of action until it worked out for me.

Chapter 4: Do the math, to get the cash

Throughout the history of our planet, human beings have always use math to solve problems. If you ever speak to any successful CEO, CFO, President, Vice President, Senior Manager or Senior executive of any business or organization they always do the math first and know the numbers. In life, you are the acting CEO and Chief Executive of your growth and success. As the Chief executive of your success, it is your duty and obligation to do the math first. When people think about super-sizing, their income people never do the math first. The average person never does the math to get the cash.

See it's hard for people to wrap their head around a million dollars. In all actuality, a million dollars isn't a lot of money in this day and age. A million dollars isn't some impossible number that you could never get to. Do the math on what necessary to hit a million. The trick is that you have to break a million dollars down into smaller and digestible doses that allows you to wrap your head around it. Math is a universal language and math is the official universal language of money. If you make 50,000 a year for 20 years, you made a million dollars. If you earn 40,000 a year for 25 years, you made a million dollars. If you make 100,000 a year for ten years, you made a million dollars.

If you make 250,000 a year for four years, guess what, you just made a million dollars. Do you get the picture that I'm painting for you? Check this out, if you create and sell a 5,000 dollar product to 200 people you're a millionaire. Sell a 2,500 dollar product to 400 people you're a millionaire. Sell a 2,000 dollar product to 500 people you're a millionaire. Sell a 1,000 dollar product to 1,000 people you're a millionaire. If you get 500 people to give you 167 dollars a month for 12 months your a millionaire.

Or if you get 400 people to give you 209 dollars a month for 12 months your a millionaire. Get 300 people to provide you with 278 dollars a month for 12 months your a millionaire. Get 1,000 people to give you 83 dollars and 50 cents a month for 12 months your a millionaire. Get 2,000 people to provide you with 41 dollars and 75 cents a month for 12 months your a millionaire. Get 5000 people to give you 16 dollars and 67 cents a month for 12 months your a millionaire. Did you get it? Did you get the picture that I just painted for you? When I decided to break down the math and see the different ways I could make a million dollars. I said to myself how can I take massive action and implement thirty or 40 of these million-dollar formulas so I could multiply my income astronomically.

The reason why I did this was simple, to supersize my income. To become a millionaire, a multimillionaire or a billionaire you have to do the math to get the cash. Every week I do weekly one-on-one, and group coaching calls with my clients. I remember one time in a group coaching call I asked the participants of that call how you would be able to come up with a million apples? I asked them three questions. Number one, is there a million apples on the face of this planet? Number two,

Where can I find these apples and who has them? Number three, come up with a blueprint to get the apples from them to me. It took me a long time to realize, but a lot of people attack this problem the wrong way. They worry about the blueprint of how they could get the apples instead of doing the math first. By doing the math, it breaks down the result, creates possibility and allows you the set massive targets. See because the only thing that happens when you start off doing your blueprint and not the math first is that you're wasting time. Whether it's apples, oranges or crispy dollar bills you have to do the math first.

From the time that you wake up to the time that you go to sleep reinforce your commitment to doing the math daily and super-sizing your income will be a reality rather than a fantasy. Increasing your revenue is more about numbers then it is about money. Whenever you're growing your capital, you have to "keep it stupid simple." I remember one time I was working with a customer at the dealership back when I used to be a car salesman. Quick little sidebar, I was the number one car salesman in my dealership, but I digress let's get back on track. The customer came in and said to me Hey Dale; I'm looking to get out of this car. My finances are all jacked up I don't have enough money for my day-to-day expenses. He told me he had the car for one month and the payments were too high. Now the car was worth about 36k brand new. I ask him two simple questions, how much you pay a month and how many months you have left?

He said I pay $1,000 a month and I have 71 months left.

Look he didn't do the math first. $1,000 a month times 72 months equals $72,000 on a $36,000 car, that's double the price. I was quickly able to come up with a complementary solution for him which helped him out dearly. Once you do the math, you can see how super-sizing your income is attainable. So figure out exactly how many clients you need, how much they need to be spending & how much you need to be making to reach your goals. Always remember to do the math and the rest will follow.

Chapter 5: Increase your cash flow

Increasing your cash flow is a substantial factor that comes into play after you have done the math and realized what's possible. When you're growing your cash flow, you want to start off first in small steps and hitting targets than in significant gaps upward. When I started out in the sales business, I was going door-to-door hunting for deals so that I could put a little meat on my skinny bones. The first thing that I did was I did the math so I can turn the increase in my cash flow into reality. Back then, I was doing a door-to-door sales job and was paid commission only, no base salary and the commission was about $200 per closed deal. On average, the salespeople that I worked with would knock on about 4 to 5 doors a day and maybe close one deal every two days. I completely hated that job, but I hated being broke and not having no money more than I hated the job.

The salespeople were making about 400 a week. I too was making approximately $400 a week until I concluded to stop acting like a little bitch and do whatever it takes to increase my cash flow. See the thing I did was I increase the amount of outflow that I was putting out, which then raised the amount of inflow that was coming in, make sense? The average salesperson knocked on about 4 to 5 doors per day. I went from knocking on 4 to 5 doors per day, two knocking on 15 doors minimum a day. I was pretty okay with sales and closing deals. I then said to myself if I could get in front of more people than I could give more presentations, and the more presentations I do, than the more deals I could close.

Immediately after I increased my outflow and the number of doors that I knocked on each day. I went from closing about two deals a week to about ten. This encounter was the first target that I set for myself. By implementing a strategic dosage of action, I was able to increase my cash flow. I did the math first and I took my income from about $400 a week to $2000. By doing the math first, I knew that if I closed eight more deals a week, that would be an additional 1600 dollars a week, 6,400 dollars a month and that's 76,800 dollars a year. I didn't switch, change or get a new job. In fact, I didn't even like the job that I had, but what I did do was come up with a way to increase my income at the position I already had. At the end of the first month, I made a little bit over $6,000. I continue to keep the math super simple and step by step track myself to over 80k that first year. I was so excited and couldn't believe that I made above 80K in 12 months.

This concurrence then showed me how important it is to use steps or increments in generating cash flow which then builds confidence and validation in your abilities. See the truth is once you quit complaining and crying and acting like a little bitch and moaning and take responsibility by increasing your cash flow it's absolutely, breathtaking the things that can happen. When you think about money, money comes to those who pay the most attention to it and use the most aggressive plans of action to get it. I spent more than a considerable portion of my life without any money, the only thing I ever did was complain about it, make excuses, and come up with reasons on why it wouldn't work for me. How things could never work for me. How the playing field was tipped in a way that wasn't in my favor. I want you to take a second right now, And think about the people around you or people that you know, that come up with reasons on why something has not happened, or reasons why something won't work out for them, are also the people who are always broke. To all my salespeople that are reading this book, you already know what you have to do.

You have to sell more; you have to close more deals, you have to give more presentations and supersize your income. Now the people who are not in sales you have to look at every conceivable way possible to add more cash flow to your life. Most importantly don't say to yourself that you cannot create more income it is 100% not right and you're lying to yourself by saying so.

It is a lie to say you can't supersize your income. If you work one job now okay cool, l get the second one. You see what I just did, that instant revenue right there. Whether you're a waiter, a dog walker, babysitting, doing your neighbor's child hair or driving a cab you have to do whatever it takes to supersize your income. Now some people made read what I just said and say, man, I'm too good to babysit or drive a cab. Okay, Dale, I have heard enough, and this doesn't seem like something that I should do at the magnitude of the individual I am. For those people who say that, the only thing that is not equivalent to the magnitude of the individual that you are is being broke. See some people try to look for ways and say things like hey man, I'm just trying to get on my feet. Well, the fastest way to get on your feet is to miss two car payments. If there's one thing I know is that broke people complain and bitch while rich people take action to get financially lit.

Look if you want money you have to do whatever it takes to get it. You can't be crying, and most of all you can't be bitching you have to come up with a plan of action, do the math and make it happen by increasing your cash flow and super-sizing your income. Most of all you have to make a commitment to yourself and commit in your abilities, to improve your cash flow and once you do so, you'll realize that it's a lot easier than you think. Your mom your dad your children your aunt your uncle's your family and your community are all counting on you to increase your cash flow and to supersize your income. Quite frankly, I know it's possible, and I know you can do it. See a lot of people have a lot of objections in life. Hey, I won't do this, I won't do that. I want you to stand up right now and say to yourself under no circumstances will I ever be broke and that I'm willing to do everything under the sun to make sure I never go broke. The people around me, deserve better, I deserve better, and I will focus all of my time and energy into doing better. See you got to put it in the air when it comes to getting financially lit. After you put it in the air, you have to reinforce it day in and day out every day and make sure that as each day passes you are taking the step closer to your end goal of super-sizing your income.

For example, if you send my company a referral on any one of the services that we provide just like that, you got instant cash flow. If you send any person or firm to purchases Ferdinand University my online sales training platform, I'll pay you 500 dollars. If you get me one of those a week, I will pay you $24,000 a year, see again that's instant cash flow. If you get me three of those a week, I'll pay you $72,000 a year. That's just from telling people around you about a fantastic product that helps people make more money. I want you to take a look at your income right now let's say you're making $30,000 a year. Just think about it, for one moment, and if you referred me three people a week for 12 months that $72,000 a year. You could write that down in your book as a win, my company and I could write that down in our book as a win, and most importantly the people that you referred to us will write it down in their book as a win. Now when you tally this up, you'll see this is what you call a trifecta. Three parties involved in one transaction, all three parties coming out making more money than what they went in with and everyone wins.

Setting up as many situations like this for yourself is a crucial way to supersize your income. Now I know that you're still getting a custom to doing the math first so let's do a little math. You're currently making $30,000 a year plus the additional $72,000 a year I'm willing to pay you that's $102,000 a year that you'll make. What that does for you, that now shortens up your timeline to a million dollars instead of taking 33 years at making $30,000 a year to reach a million I now saved you 22 years to hit that same goal.

There are so many innovative ways in this day and age to supersize and increase your income like the world has never seen before. From blogging, multi-level marketing or network marketing, internet sales, editing, shooting videos, starting a podcast or web series, they're arsenals of ways to increase income, and I don't know about you, but I'm always looking to add some additional cash flow to my portfolio. See there's a saying that you are the product of the five people that are around you the most.

So you need to surround yourself with like-minded individuals that are laser beam focused on increasing their cash-flow and supersizing their income. Now once you've improved your cash-flow you have to keep doing that, you have to continue to do the math and scale up. Kind of like when you put a water balloon on the faucet in your sink. You got to keep that water running, the more the water is running, the bigger the balloon gets until the balloon literally explodes. When that balloon explodes more than likely you'll have water all over the sink, you may even have water all over you, you may even have water literally dripping from everywhere, and that's what you want. That's what you want to do with your income; you want to have enough income and money coming in until it explodes and you have cash everywhere.

Now as you increase your income you also have to enhance your skills. See skills and income run hand-in-hand the more sharpen your skills are, the easier it becomes for you to increase your revenue. As your income starts to go up in steps, your skills go up, as your skills go up in steps, your salary starts going up in gaps. So you always got to skill-up so your income than gaps up. What I'm explaining to you now is called gaps-ups. As your income starts to gap up, so does your skills. You get more confidence in your abilities as well. I remember the first time that I made 8K in one month. My certainty and my belief in my abilities went through the roof.

Now that I knew what was possible I was a German shepherd with a bone after I got the taste in my mouth there was no letting go for me. What I then did was I continue to build my skills, I continued to skill-up, I continued to do the math, I continued changing my mind in the way I approach things and set it bigger targets for myself. I kept doing this until I was able to make $8,000 in the day now I can make four times that in an hour. Now does that speak to the magnitude of the individual that you are? However, keep in mind that I had to build up to this in steps and then gaps until it became a reality. And you will probably have to do exactly what I did or something similar. Someone can easily tell you to get rich overnight or get rich carefully but increasing your cash flow is absolutely necessary for your cash to start gapping up. If there is one thing that is for sure, that no one gets wealthy, prosperous, or financially free without increasing their cash flow first. Absolutely, no one. Anyone who is truly financially free increased is their cash flow either through the sale of some type of product or service or through the financial services industry.

The number one misconception people have about super-sizing their income is that they foolishly think that you can get wealthy or financially free from saving. You will never supersize your income or your cash flow through saving it's about having multiple streams of income all coming to you. Now I know what your thinking, that you got to either be the CEO of a company or operate your own business to really super size your income and that just isn't true. If you were to go out and look up how many people earned million dollars last year, you would see that at least 75% of those people who did it, did so working at a job. See one of the key things that you must understand is that whether you own a business or you are an employee of a company, you are your own business. I worked in the car industry for quite some time.

    The dealership didn't close my deals for me, the BDC Department who called the customers, they didn't close my deals for me, I closed my deals for me. The dealership just provided me with a decent little bit of office space but the day to day grind was me operating my duties and obligations to my family to generate an income like a business. You get what I'm saying to you? You are your own business, and your survival in the marketplace is valued by your ability to create cash flow. In order to create cash flow you don't need a business plan, or office space you just need to be 100% committed to your success. The creation of cash flow or the ability to increase cash flow is your duty in which you must find something of value that you have and exchange it with someone who's willing to pay you for it.

Chapter 6: The money is already printed, you just have to go and get it

Here is one of the smartest, simplest and genius things you could ever tell yourself that I tell myself each and every day, who will buy from me today? See I'm looking for people who have a bankroll. When I say bankroll, I'm referring to substantial pool of money or bottomless pockets. Understand that there has never been a shortage of money in the history of this planet. Even more importantly, that the money is already printed, you just have to go and get it. By telling yourself who will buy from me today? Better yet who will buy from me right now? Some people spend years building business strategies, business plans running analytics and never ask their self who will buy from me today? What this does, is it allows you to determine who has the money that you want. I want you to take a moment to think hard and write down a list of everyone that has the money or the bankroll that you want and convince them to exchange with you.

Now it doesn't matter if you're pushing a product, an idea or even a service. It doesn't even matter if you're making money better yet, you don't even need to make money. All you need to do is to find people who, one already have money, or two, have already made money and exchange your knowledge, skills, ideas or know-how with them so in return they share their money with you.

See the money is already printed you just have to go and

get it. Write down the list of the people that have your bankroll and spend as much time as you could with them. Get your mentality focus on this process. Spend every waking minute, second and hour providing those who have what you want, with something that they need. The name of the game is, give, give, give, request, and give, give, give, request. I remember when I was 23 years old and I started my first business which was my ATM Placement and consulting company. I spend almost all of my time getting in front of people who could either place my ATMs in their business or buy my consulting services that I was offering. I also made sure that I got in front of people who may not have been ready for my services but knew people who might be interested or benefit from my products and services. I also stop spending time with those who couldn't buy my products and services or refer me to people who could buy my products and services.

I would attend speaking engagements, seminars, conferences and I wouldn't waste time with the people who didn't already have money. I would scan the floor or whatever room that I'm in and do what I could to meet with the rainmakers. While I'm there, I'm not rude, I'm polite I pay attention, I smile, but I remind and say to myself and the people that I bought with me that when we leave there, we are leaving with their business and their bankrolls. We are here to find the people who will buy from me today. This should be the primary thought in your mind, who will buy from me today? Every single day, this is the most important target to have. Otherwise, if this isn't the most important target that you have, you would be wasting time, valuable time, with people who are not willing to invest their money into your products, your services, your business, and ideas.

By wasting your time with non-qualified buyers or non-qualified potential buyers, you're setting yourself up to run into a laundry list of problems and situations. So to avoid running into these unnecessary difficulties and issues make your foremost thought who will buy from me today. Now I know what your thinking, I must be a bad, no good, selfish, self-absorbed person.

If there's one thing that I realize, I'm never any of those things when I'm the provider for my loved ones. I'm never one of those things when I take my staff out for drinks, and I'm the one who picks up the tab. Or I'm the one who picks up the dinner tab, or I'm the one to take my whole team on a paid vacation. Also, no one ever thinks I'm selfish when the bills come in, or they need to borrow a few dollars. Or let's say they have an idea, and now it's time to look for funding to turn that idea into a business you won't consider me selfish, when I'm the one that's invested in them.

See if I didn't make "who will buy from me today" my number one target, I wouldn't have the cash to pick up the dinner tab. Or to pay for a vacation for my team or to pick up the drinking tab at the bar or to give you the seed capital when you decide to start up your business. This is just super-sizing your income in the purest form. Get next to the people with money and transfer the money from their pocket into yours, ethically. Have you ever heard the saying that with friends like that who needs enemies? So I want you to do this, go hang out with the people who are considered the have-nots. Who are not generating any money, and do nothing more than whine, bitch and complain. Now guess what you'll wand up becoming the same. I hope that didn't go over your head like a carry on. Who will buy from me today is one of the most powerful things you can focus on to help you save time, generate money and supersize your income.

When you focus on who will buy from me today, it allows you to manage your time better and not waste it. I give you my 100% personal guarantee that if this becomes your primary target that you will supersize your income to astronomical levels that you didn't even think were possible. I want you to ask yourself this question every day, multiple times a day, and keep asking yourself who will buy from me today until you find out who will buy from you today. After you find out who will buy from you today, do any and everything you can to get in front of them. Once you roll up your sleeves and go all-in and become committed to this concept, or to this way of thinking the money will attract directly to you like a magnet. I learned this saying when I first began working on Wall Street that you're only one deal away, regardless of your situation, your background, or even your bank account. If you have zero dollars in your bank account today and you get in front of the right person, or rainmaker, and do whatever it takes to exchange with that rainmaker, now your bank account is no longer on zero anymore. See you are always just one deal away. You have to commit, and I don't care what you do as long as you get up and do it.

You have to follow the money, whether that's cold calling prospective buyers, sending out thousands of emails, or even going door-to-door and presenting. You have to commit. Now I know there are some people out there who say well Dale, I'm not a people person like you, I don't know how to talk to people, and I don't like talking to people. I say to them well what would you rather do? Talk to people and create new deals and find the money that's out there that has your name on it or be broke and unable to provide for yourself, your family and your loved ones. You got to remember nobody likes just getting by and I'm pretty sure you don't either, so stop being a little punk ass bitch, go and get that bankroll. See by telling yourself that you don't know how to talk to people or you can't do it; you don't know how to do it, that's just the bullshit that you tell yourself to settle for being broke or something you tell yourself to justify being broke.

Remind yourself that super-sizing your income is your priority and responsibility. I want you to set big enough targets for yourself the excuses or why not, won't matter. You'll start giving yourself excuses for why you need to complete your goals and targets. See I remember a while back when I was a kid my dad used to be in love with a drop top Mercedes. My dad would always say things like goodness, that's a nice car, but I can't afford it. See with that way of thinking you're setting yourself up for failure. What my dad should have been saying to himself was not that I couldn't afford that car, but what do I need to do to afford that car and not only one but three more just like it.

See when you allow yourself to set larger targets for

yourself, not completing those targets is not even an option. You will never become the next Bill Gates, or Warren Buffett from sitting in your bedroom and not putting your foot on the gas and getting next to the people who will buy from you. Even if some of the most successful CEOs and entrepreneurs of the past decade, may have started in their bedrooms, the bank accounts didn't multiply until they decided to get out of the bedroom and get in front of some potential buyers. See when people buy your products and services, they're not actually buying just your products and services. They're buying you; they're buying your personality, their buying your commitment, and your belief in your product that it's going to benefit them or benefit their business, so they exchange their money with you.

I remember going from zero dollars in the bank to my first 200 thousand going door-to-door from business-to-business looking for potential buyers of the services that I was offering. I would say to myself each time after I would go to a business and the business owner or manager would tell me no, I'm not interested, well there's somebody out there that has a yes for me, it's just my job to go out there and find it. Now I was going from door-to-door, which I hated doing, I mean I absolutely hated it. I got no after no, after no, after no, after no, after no, after no. Eventually, after weeks and weeks of going door-to-door I said to myself if this last location says no to me then that's it, I quit and I'm done. I walked inside of a hair salon reached into my book bag, yeah I carried a book bag at that time, sometimes I still do, I pulled out a folder with a brochure that I made and pitched my services that I offered to the location owner. With my palms sweating, heart beating out of my chest, the location owner looked up at me, and he said yes, then he stuck out his hand and shook mine.

Once the owner said yes to me, he told me not only do I want your services at this hair salon I own, but I would like to add your services to all of my other hair salons. In total, it came out to about 43 hair and nail salons all together. I instantly went from having no clients, to having 43 locations along with phone numbers of some of his closet friends and family members who are also business owners that would be interested in my services as well. You must understand this wasn't something that I like doing or wanted to do, I needed to make money, so I went out there and kept grinding until I made it happen and eventually it paid off. I did hundreds of presentations to get my name out there. Oh yeah, and these presentations were for free, but in the back of my mind, I knew that the money was already printed I just had to do whatever it took to get it. See, the thing I used to get it was asking myself who will buy from me today.

The recipe I use was quite simple, and it's something that you can quickly and easily implement yourself. It doesn't matter the slightest bit what your business is, or who's your targets are, none of that stuff matters. What matters is getting in front of the people with the money.

One of the most essential skills that I learn in this lifetime is how to sell. There's a TV show that comes on called Shark Tank, they have a bunch of investors sitting on a panel and people come up and pitch their ideas, or they pitch their businesses. The very first thing the sharks, which is what they call the investors on the show is, okay great, you got a great idea, you have a great business concept, but what are your sales? When you're looking at sales, you could use a bunch of different metrics, techniques, and strategies but they are all equal to one thing, who will buy from you today.

Who has the money that will fund my business, my ideas, my products, or my services? Once you realize who will buy from you today, you have to put on your salesman hat and then close them on your products and services. Whether you have a history in sales or you're new to the game of selling it doesn't matter I can help you become a master salesman and a master closer with my online training platform called Ferdinand University. Right now, make a list, get a whiteboard write it out on the board or on the walls of your office, or room who will buy from you today. Who has the money that you need and get in front of them.

Now once you're in front of them I'll show you what to do what to say and how to close that deal and put their money in your pocket, remember, you're only one deal away from super-sizing your income. You're just one deal away for financial freedom. You're only one deal away from setting up your family's legacy, so you never have to worry about money again.

Right now if you have a shortage of money it's because you have not invested your time being around the right people, places, and the right faces and focusing on who will buy from you today. Just like I said earlier there's no shortage of money on this planet. So if you lack money, it's something that you're not doing right, go through the steps that I mentioned and you'll see getting around the capital is your best ability to get to the money. Spend your time with people who can actually buy what you're selling. The truth is, even if you're in a situation right now when you're around the people who have the money and for some reason at the end of that initial meeting you're leaving without their money. You need to sign up for Ferdinand University, and I'll make sure that problem doesn't happen again.

Chapter 7: Don't let your money just sit around

Once you start to grow and super-size your income, don't let your money just sit around. Yeah, you heard me correctly. Don't let your money just sit around. You probably think what do I mean; it's quite simple, don't let your money just sit around! See once I started to grow my income I didn't have my money just sit around I would move that money out of my day-to-day accounts which I used to conduct my regular business and transactions and put my money into separate accounts, which I will use for future deals or future investments when those opportunities arise.

Back when I was working in the FinTech space, I remember speaking to the payroll clerk about setting up some weekly deductions from my paycheck. I can't remember her name but she was a sweet girl, and I said to her, look I want you to take 30% of my income and direct deposit it into a separate personal account that I had set up. Her reply was I'm sorry, but I'm not sure that we could do that, took me about 15 minutes of convincing her, but I was able to get it done.

Now the accounts where I moved my extra money that was generated for my job, I would go through my online banking application and put little nicknames on those bank accounts like my future real estate deals, stock market funding and a bunch of other names. I realize from the people around me just by taking my money, putting it up and saving it that it wouldn't grow. That my bank account wasn't some cocoon that would allow my money to blossom into a beautiful butterfly. See one thing I know for sure is when you just have excess cash sitting around and not being multiplied or used as leverage to generate some new cash flow you get bored.

The truth is, I'm pretty sure if you're reading this you can relate, that when you get bored, your money gets bored, so you go out and do things so you won't be bored anymore. You may loan money, you may spend it, you may go out more than you need to go out, you may buy extra things that you may not need to buy, so you can't have your money just sitting around.

See I used to make money and then spend the surplus of money that I made and keep just enough money to pay my bills and operate my business. See I didn't build up the discipline to trust myself with that surplus of cash. So what I did was with the surplus money that I generated I would move into these accounts that I will use later on future deals or future investments. I was fortunate enough to learn a skill while I was working on Wall Street that taught me how to multiply the money that I already had. I learn how to navigate through the financial markets using trading and investing in an arsenal of different financial products and asset classes. So while I was working and generating my income, I would multiply that extra capital that I put aside in those accounts that were set up for future investments so I could create a new flow of profits that I didn't have to manage second-by-second minute-by-minute.

See one of the significant benefits of me pulling the excess cash or that surplus of money out of my day-to-day accounts and moving it over to those separate accounts is that my money was never sitting around. Which then made me have to get up, lace up my boots and go out and generate some new revenue. There were times when I was making more cash than I have ever made before, and I will immediately transfer it to my separate account or my brokerage account to be used later and left no money in my pockets. There were times where I had the money to pay something as simple as my cable bill or my cell phone bill, but I didn't physically have the money in my regular account, so I couldn't just pull it out of the ATM. So what that would do is make me get up and go out there and find a new referral, prospect or opportunity and close then with the utmost sense of urgency and pays my bills. Imagine that you're doing well you're making more money than you ever made before and you can't pay your bills. See by me doing this it forced me to go and get new money which is a big difference from the person who goes out and spends all their money and then they can't pay their bills.

I seen a lot of people during my life find a blueprint or something that helps them generate money, gained a little success financially and then stop doing whatever it was that allowed them to create that wealth. By not allowing myself to have cash sitting around it than forced me to move my feet and continue on the path of what was already working for me, you get what I'm saying? Have you ever watch the basketball game? You can be watching your favorite team. Or let's say your watching the star player on your favorite team go through three quarters and they're just downright terrible. Then the fourth quarter rolls around, it's getting close to the end of the game. Now when the game is on the line, and their backs are against the wall, they just transfer into a superstar performer and close the show like a champion.

Being a former athlete myself, I have also found myself in this type of situation. In fact, human beings also tend to perform better when their backs are against the wall. You notice that extra drive you find, that new ambition you see, that additional will to work harder when your back is against the wall. By me knowing this about myself, I was able to move my money, which artificially created this type of scenario of my back being against the wall so I would have no choice but to become a superstar performer. By watching some of the most successful people on the planet and some of the people who are not super successful, by the way, you can take tactics, techniques, and procedures from both of those groups of people and learn something that will help you excel to the next level. It's astonishing that I would meet people who are incredibly wealthy and they think, move and operate as if they're broke and the people who are close to broke than the wealthy operate differently.

Even to this day, you'll see people who pretend to be wealthy relaxing spending the last money to look good why the wealthy are holding their chips and grinding hard as if they got nothing in their bank account. If you don't believe me here's what I want you to do. Just hop on your phone and go on

Instagram and scroll down the timeline. I grew up in the projects and I wanted to grind hard to get out of the projects so regardless of how much money I make, I still keep that same hustle, that same grind, that same hustler's mentality to not settle in my surroundings. I spent a significant portion of my life misleading and deceiving myself. Putting a value on things that are in all actuality valueless. Until one day I realize what I was doing wrong and put in place the necessary actions to no longer mislead myself.

Even to this day when I wake up, I keep pushing as if I have $0 to my name regardless of the previous day's success. Understand this; If you follow what I'm telling you, I give you my guarantee that the same thing will happen to you. If you use your ability to think strategically, take massive action and put in the hard work and you'll find success, guaranteed. I'll repeat that if you use your ability to think strategically, use significant levels of action and put in the hard work, you will achieve success. If you repeat this process day in and day out. Day in and day out over time you'll find success. I heard one of my favorite speakers, Reginald F. Lewis, once say that it doesn't matter the slightest bit how many times you fail, if you keep pushing no matter what, keep pushing no matter what, keep pushing no matter what, and keep pushing no matter what. Eventually, the operators of the universe will say, hey you see that guy there? Something is wrong with him, and he just won't give up, he just doesn't know how to quit. How about we let up on him, and let him get this win because he doesn't know any better. By understanding the correct processes, and repeating that same process over time, you will supersize your income. Once you get this down packed and you have this instilled and ingrained into your DNA there's almost nothing on this planet that could stop you.

Did you understand what I just said? Imagine if, by repeating the same process over and over there is nothing on this planet that could affect your income. Keep in mind; it won't happen by itself you have to put in the work. Having an idea is a great thing, but an idea is just an idea if you don't put in the hard work and bring that concept to life. You can be the most phenomenal artist in the world. With the most magnificent pictures ever created in the world but if you don't announce yourself and get eyeballs on you, the world would never know. In 2008, I witness the country go through a financial crisis and became obsessed with how banks make their money which led me to come up with a business idea.

I took my idea that I had and printed up my first initial business cards and started pitching my vision until it worked out for me. I was a young kid, no experience, absolutely zero know how zero connections and zero mentors that were doing something along the lines that I wanted to do. I disregarded all of that and used explosive amounts of effort and action until I closed my first deal. After I found my early success closing my first agreement, which, gave me little extra money in my pocket. I duplicated that process so I can close more deals, and more deals, and more deals, because the more deals that I closed as I said earlier, the more money I would have in my pocket. The more money I had in my pocket, the more I could put away in a separate account to use later to generate more money.

See what I did, I used the same tactic I did with my money, with my business. When I say business, I mean the prior customers that I closed. I would go out and contact new customers who would generate new business, for me. I also took that same approach when it came to my money as well. I went out and got some new money by acquiring new customers, closing them, then putting that money off to the side. Than generating some more money by a process, I like to call stockpiling customers. Every customer that I would close and we come to terms with a transaction, I would get a least five RPOs from them of people that would be interested in my products and services. RPOs are referrals, prospects, and opportunities. This process would give me multiple new customers from my current customers which allows me to stockpile customers. See by stockpiling my customers, to get new customers, it than in-turn allowed me to stockpile my money to get more money.

See I preserved my money by putting it to the side in a brokerage account to be used later. I didn't slow up either, and I continue to operate my primary business to get more customers which overall led me to make more money, you follow me? This was the strategic discipline that I installed into myself. I then use the surplus cash that I put to the side to invest in new ventures and new businesses which created new income flows. See what I did was I don't party much, I don't drink that much. I don't go out, I don't waste money on unnecessary things that I don't need. However, there was a point in time in my past, back when I did, but I learn from it and no longer do anymore. Understand that the more money that you spend now, the less money you have to generate new wealth later.

At times you must deprive yourself of the unnecessary things that you think you need now, but in all actuality that you don't need so you can later afford anything that you want in the future. As soon as you get paid, automatically move the majority of that income into separate savings accounts which you do not touch. Since you now won't have much spending money, it will force you to focus on increasing revenue. I remember one time a female was speaking to me, and she said you seem like you do pretty well for yourself, but to me, it looks like your life is boring you don't do anything but work all day long go home wake up and work again. I didn't have any intentions of being rude, so I just said to her, I'm working hard today, so I can have my money work for me for the rest of my life.

Chapter 8: Just saving money is a losing strategy

By just saving money that is a losing strategy. You will never supersize your income by just by saving your money. I repeat you will never supersize your income by just saving your money. The only reason any sane person should ever save their money is to invest and multiply it. Unfortunately, I grew up under the impression that you should just save your money just in case something happened, or you got a few dollars put up for a rainy day. I have read tons of books on wealthy people, and every one of them never said anything about using the money that you saved to fund the repercussions of an emergency. They instead spoke about using your savings as in a vehicle to expand your reach and generating more capital. I saved my money week after week, month after month, year after year until I was able to fund my business.

I then set out to grow and expand my business which I later did after about four years of beating the pavement consistently. I then was finally able to fund my second company. Keep in mind that I was only able to do so after years and years and years of making sure that the first business model I set up was still up, running, operational and producing cash flow. I was already in the financial services field, so when I pulled the money from the primary business, I funded the sales training company it fed off of the clients I already had in my first business. So, therefore, the first business set the stage to feed the second. Then the second business set the stage to grow the primary business. See that's one of the most important things that you have to do when you're looking for additional streams income. You don't completely abandon your business model, come up with a

second stream, that's still related to the first flow so both streams of money can work hand-in-hand. I focused on my two businesses for about five years before I finally felt comfortable enough in my skin that I knew enough about the industries of finance and sales that I could start doing one-on-one coaching with people. I worked with hundreds of business owners just giving away free coaching sessions. I did tons of presentations at corporations, business conferences, networking events and charities before I decide to build a business around doing sales training and business development consulting.

After years of sharpening my skills in selling, presenting, convincing, persuading, demonstrating, negotiating, cold calling, prospecting, following up, getting internet leads, getting referrals, handling objections, closing deals and inspiring others. I got a paid speaking engagement at a college during this event they do every year called "Greek Week." I gave a speech on the DNA of success, being the to go-to person in your circle, the dangers of being average, tapping into your unlimited supply of effort and action and creating your own economy, so you are never depended on the nation's economy. The students, professors and campus staff loved my presentation so much that they purchased all of the sales training workbooks, posters and coaching sessions that were available. This completely blew up my consulting and coaching sessions, which took the consulting portions of my business to all-time new heights.

See I spent years doing the math to get the cash. I spent years of increasing my cash-flow. I spent years of getting in front of people and asking myself "who will buy from me today," and I spent years of not letting my money sit around before I was able to blow up my bank account. Understand this, It took years of discipline and following my formula of "skills times drills times will equal kills" (skills x drills x will = kills) which was the critical ingredient in me being prepared to take advantage of any and every opportunity when it presented itself. Most people miss opportunities when it presents itself because they fail to prepare. They fail to have the proper discipline, the money or courage. People don't create wealth because they play the game on a significant scale let alone make big bets on the highest levels of industries. On the other hand, super wealthy people play the game on the massive scale. Look at Donald Trump, for instance; now I know you're going to say he's a horrible president he hates particular demographics of people, but you have to understand when Donald Trump goes to play the game he plays it on the largest scale he can play on. When he bets on something, he bets on the absolute highest level that anyone can bet on. For example, if you just take a quick look at his rise to becoming the president of the United States He made a big bet on himself, and he won.

Just like the way Trump won the White House, you have to do the same thing. You have to make enormous investments in yourself not only these little tiny itty bitty little small minuscule baby portion investments in yourself. See you can't worry about not losing too much. You got to be all in when it comes to super-sizing your income. You have to be all in; you have to be 110% committed. See most people never supersize their revenue because they are already planning on the failure and they have a cutoff point. They say, hey if I don't do as well as I anticipate, that's it I'm pulling out. Now that's just one philosophy however you can never go wrong when you're betting on yourself. I remember a long time ago I attended a speaking engagement of one of the most excellent motivational speakers in the world the phenomenal and the astonishing Les Brown. At that event, I saw Les Brown hop up on the stage look at me straight into my eyes and say, you have greatness in you, and you're only limited by the limits that you set for yourself between your ears.

Now being that the goal is to supersize your income using investments, you have to, have a whole lot of cash flow. You must have some cash coming in, then put that money to the side and stacking it up. One thing I am sure of is it's easier to close a deal by being prepared when the opportunity presents itself with a couple of million dollars rather than a couple thousand. Also, you got to keep in mind that you have to build your confidence in yourself. You have to raise your confidence in your abilities and knowing that when these opportunities present themself that you've been devoted dedicated and disciplined in sharpening your skills that you will ultimately demolish and kill any opportunity that presented itself. Remember, when you are one thousand percent certain that this investment vehicle that you're looking at is the right thing and it matches up with your personality types, it matches up with your skills, ambitions and your drive, you have to go all in.

Now I don't know about you, but I'm a super big boxing fan. I absolutely love the sport of boxing, in fact, I was amateur boxer during my younger days. One of the most outstanding fighters of the last 20 years has been the boxer by the name of Floyd Mayweather. Floyd Mayweather recently had a boxing match where from invested in his own talents and his skills with persistence over time and within one fight took home north of 300 million. See super-sizing your income is just like the sport of boxing. If you look at Floyd Mayweather, for example, every single day during the last 20 years of his career he's been in the gym training, practicing, being disciplined, building his strength, working on his weaknesses, and building his capital and money. When you approach the world of investing, you have to work on developing your skills just like the professionally trained boxer does preparing for a title fight.

You got to sharpen up your skills; you have to be disciplined. You have to work on your weaknesses, and you have to move around keeping your eyes open and alert just like the counter punch boxer who fights in the middle of the ring, and he's always on defense, so he doesn't get hit, so he doesn't get hurt. He sits there patiently waiting for his opponent to open up and find the opportunity to strike. These are the key things that you must do with your money. As you train and you get your skills right when investment opportunities present them-self, you have to be like Floyd Mayweather when he's in the ring. You have to be ready, willing, proficient and able to strike with precision and accuracy. The truth is, you don't have to be the strongest to win the fight you just have to be the fastest and the smartest.

Now if you're looking to supersize your income you must have additional cash, and you must have a lot of confidence, well astronomical levels of confidence in the investment strategy in which you are looking to employ. When you know that this is the right investment for you and that this is the right vehicle for you, you got to put some skin in the game. You got to go all in and be first. In the movie "Talladega Nights: The Ballad of Ricky Bobby" a comedy movie about professional racing, Will Ferrell played a character named Ricky Bobby. In a scene, in the movie, Ricky Bobby just won a race and during the press conference said: "if you're not first you're last."

This is the exact mentality that you must have when it comes to your investments if your not first, you're last. See that's why I said you got to put your money away in separate accounts because when you decide to start your new investments, This will be the first time in a long time that you don't have that additional money at your disposal it will be tied up in that new investment.

See this is why you build that discipline of putting the money in the separate account because it's forcing you to go out and get new money as you will do when you start your second or third or fourth or fifth investment. See these are the moments when you must have complete confidence and your investments, and the previous cash flows you generated for yourself. This is great because if you're operating a new investment and this new venture takes a little bit of time to work out for you or worst case scenario let's say that it doesn't work out for you-you still have the option of relying on the previous additional streams of cash flow that you generated. At times I often find myself going months maybe even years without making any new investments or I rather spend my time making my current business and systems cash flows increase.

One and only rule is that I don't put money in any investment, any business, any idea unless it's 100% a sure thing. What I do is look for nothing but home-runs, I'm only looking for home-runs. I'm just looking for the absolute best opportunities before I plan my attack. I physically make a checklist of every single thing that could go wrong or go not in my favor before I make any investment, and if I can withstand all of the potential harmful outcomes, Then I put some skin in the game get committed and go all in. When I finally decide to go all in I'm willing to take every potential outcome even if the business goes belly-up and fails; I'm comfortable with that because I know myself and my family will be okay off the previous streams of cash flow that I created.

It has been said that the great Warren Buffett one of the greatest business minds that this world has ever seen spends all of his time looking at tons of business deals and only invest his money in sure things. Warren Buffett once said that he puts all of his eggs in one basket, but then he watches that basket.

Chapter 9: More streams equals more success

If you look in the dictionary and you look up the word stream, the textbook definition of the word stream is as follows. Definition number one "a small, River." Number two, a constantly renewed or steady supply. Let's dive a little deeper into that, a consistently renewed or steady supply. The number one difference between the haves and the have-nots is the have-nots always look to replace one stream of income with another. While the people who have, seem to generate more streams rather than substitute them. In short, the best way to describe this action is, the more streams you have the more successful you'll be. See the truth is by having more streams of income this will be the critical turning point in super-sizing your income. In fact, this concept of having multiple streams is the end all be all to super-sizing your income.

During my previous days as a young entrepreneur, I used to get knots in my stomach and complain about not generating enough income before I started to take action. I had an uncle who was a stock broker first than later became a financial adviser, and he explained to me that the problem wasn't that I wasn't making enough money from my one business, it was that my one business was only giving me one stream of income. My uncle was a financial adviser, and he's sold multiple products which gave him numerous different flows of income. He sold life, accident, and health insurance. He also sold and did asset management, annuities, 403b plans and retirement planning. My uncle also had multiple clients for each product that he sold. My uncle also owns two apartment buildings in Crown Heights, a laundromat, and the liquor company. Which in turn gave him multiple streams of income

I then set out to do exactly what my uncle told me and set up multiple businesses with multiple streams of income all flowing to my bank account. Some of my streams of income are very small like a lightly damped funnel while others are massive. The thing about all of the streams that I had they all require different levels of my focus some more than others and some extremely less than others. However, they all require a bit of my attention which makes my time very valuable. See I have more attention than I have time. Time is something that I can't get back. With that being said I made sure that I maximize every minute of every day through non-stop action and effort to entirely increase my streams. I push the envelope to make all of my streams of income a hundred times stronger. Each day, I wake up, I'm incredibly grateful for every flow that I have and pay respect to those streams by giving them my attention. Some people wake up, and they complain about their financial situations, but the truth of the matter is complaints don't solve problems, solutions do.

Like I mentioned earlier one of the critical things, well, preferably one of the crucial mistakes that people make when looking to generate more streams, they get rid of their primary income and try to get a new stream of income, rather than having multiple income streams running parallel together. Another thing people tend to mess up on when trying to add various streams is they create a second stream that has nothing to do with the first stream. They also lack knowledge on the second stream of income that they attempted to generate. For example, if I were to run a business like a barber shop I would rent the chairs to other barbers, that's one stream. The second stream will be something that runs parallel to the barbershop like selling brushes or selling hair products in the barber shop and on the barber shops website. The third stream would be to put an ATM inside of the barbershop and make money on withdrawal fees when people go to pay for the haircuts. The fourth stream of income would be to put a vending machine inside the barbershop so when people are thirsty or want a snack, I get paid again. See what I did there? I just gave you a quick example of how to have multiple streams of income work with one another. Whenever you're looking to create that second stream of income, make sure that it coincides with that first stream. So the drizzle or the flow from one will then drip over into the second stream.

The most important takeaway you need to get from creating multiple streams is whenever your creating a second flow don't just stop and forget about the first one. Follow what I'm saying don't build that second stream of income too far off from the first. When you create a second stream of income, and you put all of your attention, focus and dedication on that second stream and then neglect the first flow the only thing that happens is the original one is going to dry up and than you'll be right back down to one stream. See how that works. Now the second one that you started doesn't produce as much as the first one initially did, now you have a loss of income, understand what I'm saying? Always remember, when you add that second stream still focus on the first one. I can't say that enough because time and time again I have friends, colleagues and even on a few occasions business partners that this happens to.

Another key trick that you have to keep in mind is that you have to play tennis with your business. Now I know what you're about to say. What do you mean play tennis with my business Dale? Don't worry, I'll tell you. You must make sure that all of your current customers, clients or consumers are aware of your second stream of income and your second business. Send your customers from your first business over to the second one and do the same thing vice versa. Make sure that the customers of your second stream of business are aware of your first stream and transfer customers there as well.

See if you want to continue to expand you must create parallel flows, you don't have to get a new job. You don't have to switch your current position or do any of that stuff. Take a moment and think about your main stream of income. Think about things that work with it and that run parallel to that business in any way and then use those things to create additional streams of income. During your time off from work use that time for self-improvement and use that time as blocks that allow you to zero in and work on your ability to focus increasing volume to those additional streams of income and transferring your customers between them. If you do business with someone and they buy one of your products or services from you, recommend your other products and services that you offer as well from your other companies.

Keep in mind that you must take a lot of things into consideration before to ever decide to leave any stream of income no matter how large or how small. These are the same principles that you must apply even when you are dealing with your customers. Never walk away from customers that you have done business with especially when these are the customers who got you into the spot that you're in. See when I ran my ATM business I came up with other ways to generate streams of income all within that same business. I place my ATMs in locations like stores, gas stations, malls, hair salons and any high-traffic place that I could put an ATM at and I did. I thought of ways that would benefit both customers and business owners.

The name of the game is as you win make sure the people around you succeed as well that way no one loses. When I initially started my first business, every business that I went into didn't want to put my ATM's in their locations, so I had to improvise ways to create additional streams of income such as offering consulting services for my current and potential customers and even my non-customers which later became customers. I then leased out my terminals that weren't in used. I also charged a premium fee for my consulting services. Creating new streams of income allowed me to build my business, my mentality and myself. Throughout my experiences in life, there has been no single thing that has helped to build my self-esteem, self-trust and self-assurance like building multiple streams of income.

Always keep in mind when building multiple streams of income for yourself, you must remain devoted, dedicated, and discipline to complete a monumental task like super-sizing your income. Remember the first thing you got to do is increase your cash flow after you improve your cash flow, get those additional streams of income rolling, then take that extra money move it over to the separate accounts. Save it up until you have enough money to invest. Then you put some skin in the game when you have a potential home run in front of you. Once you find these home run investments, use them to create additional flows of income for yourself. Then focus on increasing your cash flow in that new venture. Save up that new surplus of cash and put it into a side account. Then save it up until another home run appears before you again and repeat this process again and again and again until you supersize your income and win.

Chapter 10: Repetition is the mission

Look by now you should understand that it is 100% possible for you to supersize your income. Better yet, you now know the exact formula and blueprint on how to do it. The only thing you need to do now is to take action and remember that the mission is repetition. You have to repeat the same process of the steps that I laid out for you over and over and over as you breakthrough levels of your income barriers like a sledgehammer through sheetrock. Now there's a bunch of different people out there who will give you a bunch of different advice, but I'm here to tell you that if you stay super focused and work on repeating the process, I outlined in this book, you will transform your income to new heights.

Now if anybody tells you anything different like you can supersize your income overnight they're a liar and don't forget chapter two, be careful where you get your advice from. Remember just like anything in life you have to make sacrifices one of the first sacrifices you should make is that old outdated middle-class unworkable mentality and game plan. You have more than enough tools to supersize your income, and you deserve it, your family deserves it, your community and your loved ones deserve it, so I asked you why not? There's no point in living life if you're not achieving your goals and enjoying life to the fullest potential. I come from the school of over-promise and then over deliver which was a valuable lesson I have learned from one of my greatest mentors Grant Cardone. With that being said I promise you if you follow every step that I laid out for you by the letter I guarantee you that you will supersize your income.

Another important thing that you are definitely going to have to sacrifice is, the wrong peoples perception. You're going to have to sacrifice other people's perception of how you should spend your time. Or others people's opinion of how you should spend your time to have fun. I remember on numerous occasions people would say, Dale you're boring you don't ever want to go out with us, you don't want to hang out with us, travel, go on vacations, go out for drinks. Now there's nothing wrong with any of those activities, but for me personally, I was just too committed on building financial freedom for myself that I couldn't allow myself to be distracted with anything other than that during the beginning stages of my quest.

A good indicator that you're doing something right and that you're heading in the right path is when the people nearest to you say things like damn we hardly ever see you anymore or my personal favorite is, damn all you do is work, and we barely see you. I want you to keep in mind while you're on your journey to creating massive wealth, and super-sizing your income be careful of the people who try to convince you that you don't need to do so. Some people may even say the goal that you're trying to achieve isn't even achievable. However, the truth is, that it is feasible and the journey to creating massive wealth and super-sizing your income is a journey worth taking and it's one of the most important missions of your life. Your trip to super-sizing your income will show you that you may have limited number of skills at your disposal. See when you have a limited number of skills that may increase your fears of super-sizing your income because you don't know the outcome of what will happen.

Fear comes from the lack of knowing something, from the lack of not knowing how a situation will play out before it happens. So you become fearful of such a scenario. However, the trick is, the more skills you have or, the more you increase your skill-set, the lower your fears become, see how that works. The more skills you build up, the smaller your worries will go. In the beginning, I found out that I knew nothing about networking, connecting with people, building trust, communicating efficiently and didn't have any personal confidence. I didn't know anything about selling; I didn't know anything about pitching a product, marketing, prospecting, closing deals, cold calling, following up, getting referrals or running, growing and expanding a business. I started out knowing absolutely nothing, let alone managing or dealing with money.

When I finally muscled up enough courage to invest in myself. I started to build my survival skills in the marketplace. For once in my life, I took a leap of faith with my education. I decided what I would learn, study and master. I took a leap of faith with studying some of the masters of the marketplace by reading hundreds of books on selling, finance, business, attitude building, influencing, persuading, building rapport and winning friends. I even took courses and join a public speaking club which allowed me to become a master at public speaking, giving presentations and leading meetings. I learned how to dissect successful people, business owners, entrepreneurs and duplicate the models that work for them and implement them into my business immediately. I went through a few steps in this book one of them being "increasing your cash-flow" and another being "who will buy from me today." Between these two steps, 87% of people will fail. I spend almost all of my time focusing in on these two steps for years. Also, I spend a great deal of my time getting lethal in the skills department on whatever skills I lacked.

For once in my life, I started to gain a little success, and my beliefs in my abilities began to rise gradually. As my belief and my knowledge started to expand so did my confidence in myself and my overall level of comment to increase my abilities further. After going through a period of repeating my successes I started to feel good about myself. In fact, I started to feel really, really good about myself. Over time, my immediate circle of pairs and people they I associated with became extremely judgemental of me. Not only am I'm so sure that this will happen to you I'll give you my promise that it will happen to you. See here's the thing, you have to mentally prepare yourself for when the people around you start to do this. Remember this, the people around you didn't change their philosophies, views, ambitions, and goals, you did. So this is something that you must expect because I hate to say it, but really I don't hate to say it, you have to know that some people only want to see you do but so good. There is people out there that don't want to see you do better than them. In fact, some people even consider you a threat once you start doing better than them. I remember when I started to spend more time focusing on becoming a better person and evolving myself so that I can achieve that next level of my life.

A close friend that I had at the time said to me, do I have a problem with him because he noticed that I haven't been coming around as often. Did I have some animosity towards him? I explain to my good friend at the time, that just because you don't see me as much anymore doesn't mean that I'm focusing my energy on you. In fact, it's not even about you, It's about me wanting to do something magnificent to achieve that next level and accomplish a big goal and target that I set for myself, so I isolated myself and got committed to my goals which has nothing to do with you. See the thing that happened was by me wanting to improve myself my former friends felt threatened that we weren't any longer on the same wavelength. We were no longer on the same level I developed a mental plan and then put that idea into action, while my friends were still going with the flow of whatever day the day activities came his way. If you want to supersize your income as much as an asthmatic person intends to breathe, then you have to change the people, the places and the faces that you associate yourself with. That doesn't mean you just throw those people away that you currently have in your life. The only thing you really need to do is just add more people of value into your life. Over time the associates from your past eventually disappear as they realize the things that interest you and the things that interest them are no longer the same. This again is something that I promise you unmotivated people don't tend to associate with people that are motivated, it just doesn't happen. In fact, you being a go-getter is what will actually annoy them, and then they will be the ones that distance themselves from you.

If you're looking to supersize your income you have to get around the right people, you must reach up with your relationships. "Have you ever in your life heard the saying" if you're the smartest person in the room you need to find yourself a new room? That's a very powerful and true statement; I actually like to take it a step further. If you find yourself being the person with the most money in the room you need to find yourself a new room. I guarantee you that you will not make it if you don't change the people around you, if you do not change the people that you associate with you will not make it. I want you to take a few moment and think about the most successful people in your area, your town, your city, your state and your region of the world.

Now all of the people that you thought about create a list of them. Now I bet you that the list of all these people that you just made have a few things in commend. Most than likely their goal oriented, motivated, dedicated, discipline and don't complain about their mishaps and misfortunes. Now, let's say you were able to get next to these people. Which is something that you should commit to doing anyway. You happen to tell anyone of them, I'm taking some time out to improve myself, and I'm getting committed to providing a better life for my family. More than likely they'll tell you that you can do it, great, it is possible, and for you to move forward in the process of doing it. What they will not do is give you reasons why not to do it like that little voice does in your head, or say something like your friends and family tell you, hey if it was that easy then everyone would be doing it. The truth is they would probably tell you hey we're doing the same thing and here are a few things that I did that made me successful.

See now you have a list of people that are your targets which you need to surround yourself with. People who have reached great heights and levels of success in their lives like helping other people become successful and tend to surround themselves with other people who are like-minded and ambitious as well. If you're not surrounded by the type of people that you need to be surrounded by right now, stop whatever you're doing and get those people in your life. I spent countless hours working on improving myself and finding the right people to be around. Just like I did, you should go out and find the right people to bring into your life, go to seminars, conferences, workshops, networking events, coaching sessions, public speaking clubs, mastermind groups and training programs.

Seek them out and find the people that if you get next to them, they could ultimately blow up your business or completely blow up your life. Don't waste your time and money on things that don't matter like expensive purchases of unnecessary items. Instead spend your time and money investing in your absolute best asset you can invest in, yourself. When investing in your number one asset which is yourself, there should be no limits on what you're willing to spend on your self-improvement. Do whatever it takes, if you got to sell something, borrow money, or get a second job.

Do whatever it takes to raise the capital to invest in yourself. Always remember to think big you not playing in the minor leagues or on the junior varsity team anymore. You're playing in the major leagues, and you're playing with major players, and you're looking to supersize your income on a massive level you're not looking to just get by on the nine-to-five check to check the type of salary. If you follow the steps that I laid down in this booklet in the exact order in which I laid them out you will come across a few things. The first thing that you'll come across is this isn't the most natural thing to do. The second thing is that it's quite easy once you get the ball rolling. The third and most important thing is that you will accomplish and achieve more than you ever thought was possible.

Now I don't know if any Average Joe can supersize their income I can't tell you that, but I can tell you that you can supersize your income. You took the first step in that process. You went out and bought a book on super-sizing your income. There's a reason why you picked up this book because you wanted more out of life. Your ready to beat that feeling that you got in the pit of your stomach of knowing you could do bigger and better things knowing that you could achieve more. Your ready to perform at the maximum level in which you know you could perform on. You have to remember that you have greatness in you.

Also, that great people make great decisions. For example, there is no decision more exceptional than deciding to invest in yourself and improve your quality of life for you and your family, and you did exactly that. You made an excellent choice when you picked up this book. See I know that you know it's possible and I also know that you can do it if you just do precisely word for word what I laid out in this book and never give up. The only thing you will have to do is just keep coming back to this book, keep this book in your pocket, your book bag, in your car or near you at all times so you can quickly revert to it everyday. This allows you to remain supercharged and reignite that fire within you to succeed. Understand, exactly where you are right now in this moment, what step you're currently working on. What's the next step and where you need to be? This book is the perfect blueprint and roadmap for you to supersize your income and achieve your maximum potential. If you ever start drifting off target, I need you to go through this book again and get back on target. Follow these easy-to-do strategies I laid out for you. Keep my advice and this book with you at all times. Share this book and the information within it with your friends. Build a CEO roundtable, a peer to peer, group, a success-team, or executive roundtable. This will allow you to develop some friendships with fellow entrepreneurs and like-minded people.

    I truly and honestly know that if you follow these step, you will find success in super-sizing your income. Once you pump up your revenue, I want you to call me up and let me know. In fact, make sure that I'm one of the first people that you let know. I'll be thrilled that you were able to reach your next level and level up. My goal is merely to make sure that people are winning and succeeding in life. One of those major components of your life is your finances. You can decide just to get by, and live check to check but aren't you tired of doing that haven't you done that long enough. I want to lead you to the path of super-sizing your income and generating surpluses of money which then allows you to influence others sincerely your friend, Dale H. Ferdinand.

About the author

Dale Ferdinand is an investment manager, sales expert, sales trainer, keynote speaker and author. He is most known for developing customized sales programs for various organizations of all sizes and has helped thousands of people and organizations worldwide. Large financial institutions, companies, entrepreneurs, non-profit organizations, and individuals use his training platform and systems to increase their dominance in the marketplace. He has given keynote speeches to audiences both on a national and international stage on topics such as sales, business, finance, motivation and managing investments. His explosive levels of energy and his humorous and take-action delivery keep audiences entertained, intrigued, and involved.

Ferdinand runs two companies a sales training and consulting company and an investment management company. He has written several books. One of which has been released and a few upcoming titles to be released to inspire those who want to achieve massive success: Financially Lit (2018), The Science Of Closing A Deal (2018) The Ferocious Salesman (2018), and Taking Massive Action, (2018). Ferdinand is always pushing the envelope to bring innovation to the world of traditional sales and sales based solutions; he launched a state-of-the-art, virtual sales training center, www.FerdinandUniversity.com, The author is also heavily involved in community outreach focusing on educating youth groups and organizations on sales, financial literacy and managing their money. He currently resides in the New York with his daughter.

www.ingramcontent.com/pod-product-compliance
Lightning Source LLC
Chambersburg PA
CBHW050014230526
45470CB00003B/970